We keep memories of what we looked like in photograph albums … But where do we keep the memories of what we were thinking at the time? Please keep your thoughts in these books as if they were your own journals. Or cut them up and sticky tape them into something else, to keep memories of your mind forevermore.

CLARE-ROSE
TREVELYAN
YONGHO
MOON
THE BOOK
WITH
NO STORY
Young
Philosophers

THE ONE THING & ANOTHERS
Young
Philosophers

CLARE
WHY IN THE
WORLD
ARE WE
HERE?
Young
Philosophers

CLARE-ROSE
TREVELYAN

YONGHO MOON

THE FAKE DICTIONARY

Young Philosophers Series Vol. 4
A Muddle of Meanings

RedWoolEditions

Young
Philosophers
RedWoolEditions

How to Use This Book

1. Pick your favourite letter of the alphabet.

2. Read the new, made-up meaning for an old word. You may want to wonder about what we can change in this world, what we cannot and who decided this and when?

3. Draw the new meaning in and among the photos of the author's grandmother's old things on the accompanying page, as per the example for the letter A.

4. Collect a few more words beginning with that letter, write them down and develop your own new meanings for those words. You may want to wonder more about 'change' as you write and draw. You could wonder about how you could change your mind. Or if a ghost could change their mind. Or how about, could a ghost make you change your mind? Or if a ghost could make a GHOST TRAIN in a theme park? Keep all your thoughts in a journal.

I had some spare time
on Tuesday afternoon,
so I made up some new
meanings for some
old words.

Can you help me finish
this book by drawing
the new meanings?

I've done the first one.

Astrologist

Someone who looks for magic in between metal and fire

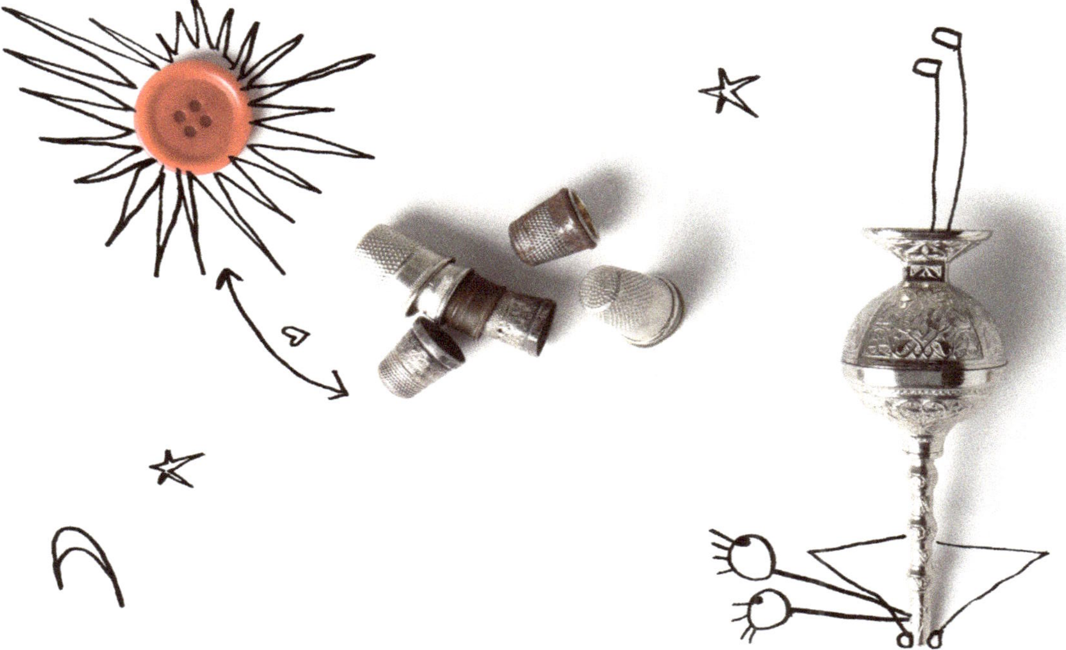

The moment the sun hits the fingertips of the moon's dreams

Chameleon

A hyena who slow dances to the sound of invisible saxophones

Daisy

An orchid with wings she
stole from a dishwasher

The feeling that something brilliant is about to happen

Fiasco

A choice between luck and fate

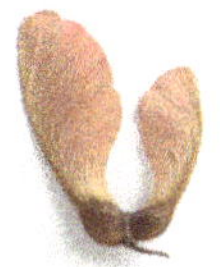

Gambler

Someone sneaking
through a labyrinth
in stilettos at dawn

Harlequin

The one who places
coincidences in your path

Illustrator

A waitress who sees faces
in wooden floorboards

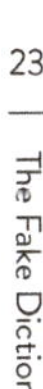

Juggler

A memory that touches the senses but doesn't stay long enough for anyone to actually remember it

J

When creatures reconcile
over a mutual dislike for
a bad meal

An antique coffee machine
made of 13 teapots, a turquoise
giraffe and seven zips

Magic Carpet

A bed that keeps your nightmares
in daydreams and makes them
apologise to you

M

Noise

The supernova inside tear drops
that makes your friends rush
to your side

Octopus

A piece of dust who thinks
she's too small

Pyrotechnic

I am a home-made dragonfly
I believe in everything

An extremely unique and
dazzling creature, who knows
exactly how to live life

Rapscallion

The song she sang when she
realised that she was only using
fear to protect her love

Side-show

A secret sparkling place they escape to when the streets are overcrowded with atrociously mind-numbing art

Young Philosophers |

Television

A blueprint of triangular paintings that prove that aliens exist

Ultraviolet

Six people thinking the
exact same thought at the
exact same time

Young Philosophers

Vagabond

A traffic light that does backflips every time the rain touches a broken heart

Wildebeest

Someone who finds strange
things in strange places
and moves them to other
strange places

Xebec

A story that inspires another story

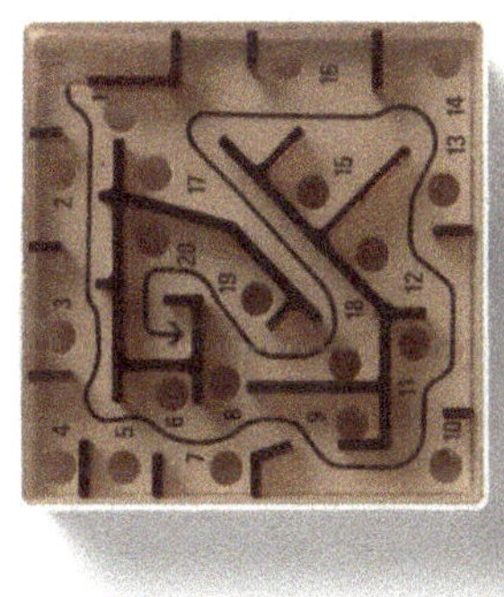

Ylang-Ylang

An art deco rocket full of lost
stories, buried deep beneath
thieves market

Y

A nomad who gives costumes
to creatures trapped in stillness,
in order to help them move

That was my
Fake Dictionary.

You can make
one up too if you
like. After all,
isn't everything
just made up?

CLARE-ROSE
Author

Clare-Rose Trevelyan believes that if all our stories were told, and all of our stories were listened to, we would find ourselves in a more gentle existence.

Her particular love is to get kids thinking about how they are thinking and wondering about why they are wondering, by weaving the questions of eternity through her collections of books.

She collaborates with as many friends as she can, in as many ways as she can, so that the stories end up mirroring a hypnotic, vivid, bouquet of truths.

She likes mysteries and doing absolutely nothing at all with her family and friends, for days and days and days on end.

If you want to stay in touch with Clare, sign up to her newsletter at www.clare-rose.com

If you want to buy any of Clare's books go to www.amazon.com/author/clare_rose

YONGHO MOON
Illustrator

Yongho Moon lived in South Korea before coming to Australia, first to Sydney and then to Melbourne. He has many talents, including skills as an engineer, but his passion is visual contemporary arts and design. His work has been shown both in Australia and South Korea where his media art has been projected on the giant facade of Seoul Square. He loves collaborating with Clare who he says offers him the freedom to develop ideas in his own way.

RED WOOL EDITIONS
Publisher

Red Wool Editions is a publishing company dedicated to unravelling the philosophical thoughts of kids, by taking them through enchanting stories, twinkling soundtracks and accompanying educational packages for parents and teachers. Our aim is to encourage young readers to create their own stories and open up family discussions on how they want to live their life and why. If you want to learn about forthcoming publications subscribe to www.facebook.com/redwooleditions

THE YOUNG PHILOSOPHERS SERIES

The Young Philosophers Series is intended as a place children can explore philosophy by doing it, rather than by being told about what it is and isn't.

At Red Wool Editions, we believe that children are natural philosophers and so we have started our first series exploring the complexities of oneself, contradiction, the thoughts of others, change, the meaning of life and senses of place. The books focus on the basic elements of storytelling as we venture further into the universe of your thoughts and eventually, your stories.

To find out more about philosophical journaling and other books by Red Wool Editions visit clare-rose.com. You'll also discover our upcoming theme park of activity books that show you how to turn your wonderings into your stories and how those stories may come to both reflect and shape our spellbinding lives.

THE FAKE DICTIONARY
Young Philosophers Series Vol. 4
A Muddle of Meanings

Written by Clare-Rose Trevelyan
Edited by Josey De Rossi
Designed by Futureinform

Published in 2023 by Red Wool Editions
Copyright © Clare-Rose Trevelyan and Futureinform 2023
ISBN 978-1-925864-22-9

Mailing Address
Red Wool Editions
PO BOX 8175 Subiaco East WA 6008
www.redwooleditions.com

Visit the author's website
www.clare-rose.com

Young
Philosophers
RedWoolEditions

www.ingramcontent.com/pod-product-compliance
Lightning Source LLC
Chambersburg PA
CBHW050045040726
47599CB00015B/1805